Gentle Haunts

Gentle Haunts

A COLLECTION OF POETRY

Andrea Reynolds

St. Louis, Missouri

Dedicated to my mom, Barbara

Contents

Thank you
to Steven Schreiner and Shane Seely, my MFA mentors
to Sarah McCartt-Jackson for her wise edits
to Cathy Wood for her expertise in graphic design
to my colleagues who prop me up—John, Margo, and Jen
to my sons and Don, especially Don
who daily convinces me to continue creating
& as always, thank you for reading.

Introduction

This collection of poetry is a reflection from an old soul with a youthful heart. The poems explore the depth of life and loss. They celebrate simple moments, and what is hidden there.

City Life

I was born in the city amidst excitement and sorrow.
laughter and tears—that was a loud day.

in the brick flat; the bungalow; the ranch—life unfolded. smells of yeast
and car exhaust floated over the linoleum; the hardwood; the carpet.
the powerful passion of innocence fueled the hopeful. feeling the freedom
of summer vacation, school boys howled coyote joy. in ash-pits
children hid while others ran through the alleys chanting jump rope rhymes.
whistles called; streetlights flickered; siblings yelled.
those who ate dinner disappeared
for a while. in tattered clothes, we gathered on stoops
blaring music and spitting seeds
at barefoot cousins; stickball tired; dripping sweat.

angst crawled in windows; climbed fire escapes; rebelled loudly.
shared struggles bound oneness. temptations nudged something more.
in bars; in gangways; in tiny apartments my black eyeliner squinted
with each inhale. entangled life leaked into dreams.

in a low car; a white truck; a city bus, people rocked to and fro mumbling
the wrong words. everyone changed. reserved talked of philosophy;
injustice demanded reform; rejected revisited religion.
worked swing shifts; two jobs; overtime aged the body. couples
discussed what to have for dinner. some feared
the growing darkness.

excitement and sorrow stared at the same sky.
laughter and tears—and the newborns sang.

Eating over the Sink

The shot glass on my windowsill
announces the morning.

I don't mind eating over the sink
rinsing the fragments
of peeled shell. Noticing
the damn deer stripped
the bark off the branches
of the sandcherry tree.
Most of its limbs
dead on the grass.

With the precision
of calligraphy, I lace the salty
confetti contrasting
the crumble of the yolk
and the smooth white.

Soon the fawns will
with trembling legs
maneuver the chain-link
by the deep storm drain
where they seem
to begin their young
journey.

Two years passed
the willow didn't survive
the meals ravished
the feathery leaves
the waving branches.

Feeling a strange twinge
I picture last year's young
deer in the metal
and concrete dangers
of my world—maybe
hungry for life.

Splitting Wood

He folds grief
into himself.

Placing the wood
on the chopping block's edge

the wind's breath blowing
one thousand miles.

His watery eyes read the grain.
Ax swings, knees bend.

The cut topples off into a pile
next to the block. How heavy

his life is. Fibers
split apart.

Nothing whole except
the work before him.

Where Dreams Take Place

Though I'm nearly 100 years old,
most of my dreams
take place in my childhood
flat. It doesn't matter
the premise.

Last night, I was 75
bickering with my skinny husband
over watering the lawn, but I
was in my 7-year-old bedroom.
Bright wallpaper with petals
shaped like teardrops spinning
pink and orange.

Tiny lime green tiles flew
off the fireplace.
The hairline crack in the plaster
edged toward my sister's bed.
And I was yelling, Stop
watering the grass.

Sunset With a Heron

You and I are different.
You believe every sunset
is miraculous.

But some nights, layers
of clouds ink-blotted
and bruised collapse on me.

You enjoy spending money and throwing
parties, and I resent having to say, No
let's not have people at our house.

It is not a mistake to camouflage myself
by pretending to understand
relationships.

And another thing, I'm quite sure
you don't listen to my impoliteness
even though your head nods up and down.
There are limits to your sympathy.
I would rather search the evening sky
for the solitary Great Blue Heron's
return, stoic and stern.

Cautiously waiting, motionless
and calm. The Heron's shadow
wades near the shore.

Follow the Bend in the Road

Maybe we live in a small town
near the bend in the road. Old utility

poles, draped with sagging wires. Glass
insulators suspend the cable above the wood.

The Ozark foothills roll
to the edge of the rocky limestone bluffs.

Straight holes scarred the bluff
where dynamite dropped down

into the formation. Sparse evergreens
in the shallow earth crown the ruddy cliff.

Some burnt orange trees and sycamores
grow through barbed wire.

One field of hay is baled
leaving dried remains and bare soil.

Behind the prairie grass, the smaller
bushes strangled by honeysuckle

hide an abandoned outbuilding.
In the next field, winter wheat begins.

Still, I'm Gonna Miss You

Remember how purposefully
　　the rain fell over the lake,
　　　　like it knew what it was doing.

Rain anticipating sullenness.
　　We were playing chicken foot
　　　　Dominoes, listening to

George Thorogood's "One Bourbon,
　　One Scotch, and One Beer"
　　　　or something from the

Rolling Stones'
　　Between the Buttons.
　　　　And layers of sky

dripped dreams and sanity.
　　You were wearing glasses
　　　　resting your hand on my lap

showering grey goodbyes
　　to the rocky, sympathetic shoreline.
　　　　Never wanting to leave.

Scavenger Finds a Body

Bloated and bobbing near the undergrowth
the body lagged against the shore.

Landing near the marsh marigolds,
a scavenger—dark pinkish legs,

with sharp talons. The scavenger
petrified at water's edge.

Hooked beak bowed down, a sign
of weariness. Only one or two pecks

before the swell pushed the
sour smelling flesh beyond reach.

The turkey vulture watched again,
and again, as the dead teased his hunger.

Unwilling to move, hours dragged.
Be willing, be ruthless, conquer.

Standing in Promises

1. We're close to the
ground. Don't fit
with polite families.

From the bottom
up, earthy. Longing
for the words, the music.

Mornings of sunlight
in the garden
listening to mama
sing. She was
standing in
promises—
Come on now
give it out.

She is going,
going to catch
a song.

2. Searching for
the tonic of lyric
and language.

Afternoons lost
franticly sweeping
life warm.

Barn dances,
tin pan, gambled
or carved a place.

Still quaint and lacking,
not a personal elixir
nor a remedy.

Whatever muse we've got,
we put it over our backs
or tie it to our soul.

3. Last night, music's
Mother Maybelle wailed
outside my window.

I belong weary, yearning
to return somewhere
I've never been.

A long time traveling,
feeling for the shallow
ground. Without promises

she beckons, but I don't
understand how to follow
the dead back home.

My Butterfly

I keep a butterfly in my pocket.
Glowing, softly fluttering
next to my chest.
When a second one barely
landed on my wrist
to taste the cotton
of my shirt,
and the hairs
on its wings
vibrated the stillness.

Everyone asked,
Is that your butterfly?
No, this one is too sassy
and too sarcastic.
But I sensed
everyone
did not know
the personality
of butterflies
so I said, *Yes.* And
I said, *How summered,*
how lovely,
peaceful,
and
fairy
dusting.

One Thing

Consider; some people depart this world
without realizing their one thing. Maybe
it's fleeting like mid-night dancing,
or maybe it's eternity like love
or truth. But, whatever your one thing is,

you have to find it. Face it. Proclaim it.
Whisper it, or ugly cry it, you must. When I was a kid
my one thing lived inside of me, nourishing my heart
and soul, getting stuck as a lump in my throat
and it will return when I least expect it

and it will matter deeply. I search the raindrops
clinging to the window. I pick up a leaf, hoping
to find cursive on its veins. If I could hold a newborn
or decipher laughter, maybe it would be.
Maybe, there is time for faint exclamations

almost forgotten by the working,
running, barely getting by, frenzied life.
My solace, writing on lined paper, the possibility
of language. A clue to consider when there is a time,
a place, a purpose for my one thing.

Trembling

The blue spruce trembled
against a clear sky.

Sections of branches ridge
and swell, slight and other worldly.

Needles stiff, a sharpness
of grief hiding pain.

We're not supposed to hear
the soft white powder

cling to the gray, green,
blue, pointed twigs.

Settling into equilibrium
the boughs begin to lag.

An unrecognizable gasp
of something lost

in the trembling
of life.

The Geese Return for You

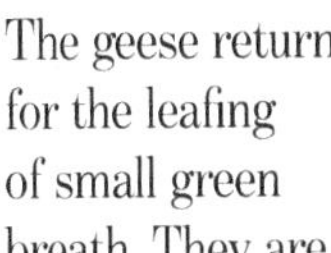

The geese return
for the leafing
of small green
breath. They are
heading home.

You don't have
to tell me about loss
or emptiness. I'm
willing to listen
but I don't need to know.

Geese aren't solitary,
and I want that for you.
Letting the breeze flow
over your body. Miles
that drown twilight.

Offering your wings
open to the sun.
There is a shape of you
in the evening sky, finding
peace in the depth of being you.

Creek Glass and Fossils

You wade the creek
gathering glass

and fossils. The glass
you flip in your hand

noting the edges.
But the fossils you

hold up to the sun
study each angle.

Warm shallow seas
covered mollusks

millions of years
before. The coiled

shell, screw-shaped
weathered and oxidized

yellow brown. Unearthed
after sediment accumulated

recording life. The fossils
 belong to the earth. Most days

you leave them, but you
always pocket the glass.

His Boots

At three thirty, he's
in a high-vis shirt
driving his truck home.

Kick off
thick soled
boots by the door.

Brotherhood.
Steel-toed years
caked with clay.

His threadbare
overalls stiff with
sun, rain, perspiration.

Buckles and straps
drape across
the linoleum.

Let the shower rinse
away the earth and sweat
uncover the man.

Third Generation

My husband didn't want our son
to follow in his footsteps.

Things were different. A simpler time
welcoming wind and work as religion.
The calling of the quiet clouds,
stars, sky, harmony of the soul,
the living air, emptied of people.

Thinking of my husband's doctors
urging him to find employment
which rests the body
yet the son continues.

I see him leaning on a rusted fence post,
stooping to pick up a stone.

Maybe he feels alone
in the charm of toil
and worldly struggles.
Neither the aching joy
or the wandering
peacefulness christens
his bearing. It is something
else carrying him home.

Midnight in Our Kitchen

I trudged in at midnight
after a ten-hour shift.
My son and my husband welcomed
me with lighthearted cheering.

These two, bristle faced
construction workers
were in the kitchen
drinking and discussing

which acquaintance
will be laid off next.
My son kicked out a chair,
Have a beer, join us.

The apprentice,
and the journeyman.
Both with rough hands,
one with jittery legs.

Usually, they bickered
over taxes and the economy,
but tonight, they laughed
and drank together.

The younger recalled
being tethered by a
harness to the umpteenth
floor for minimum wage.

How much silica has the older one
inhaled while drilling concrete?
His knees ached in the winter air
as the interstate flyover was attached.

Together, we were drinking
beer. Friday, at midnight
in our kitchen.

Just Another Day

His desk, a weathered shop table,
thick wooden slab. Near the far-right corner
a plate sized silver tin filled with screws,
bolts, rivets, and washers. On the slab,
in a random pattern (as if a child dropped
a handful of jacks) are five sets of pliers.

The risers and downcomers reach
from the HVAC to the top of the drum.
The desk faces a wall with thumb tacked permits
and inspections slips. This is where he
unscrews the small metal cup atop the green
Thermos, pours a cup of coffee, and begins.

Migration

Such a bitter damp day.
Running to my car
I hear a flock of birds
overwhelm the tree.
Up roaring prattle
continuous chatter
no other listening.

I linger in anticipation
for the migration.
Yearning to see them
soar united and abruptly
divert direction. I marvel
at the transitiveness
of beauty.

Periwinkle Carpet

Once a year, the weeding
Germander seedwell
carpets the emerald grass
inviting the bare footed young
to run across cool fields.

Perennial coin-leaf, open
their small-faced droplet
flowers, low growing
blanket of bright periwinkle.

Summer vanishes spring,
single and frail. Weakening
roots at the plant's nodes.
Short-lived memories
mocking life.

Eddie

A year before I attended his funeral
Eddie kissed me in our second-grade coat closet.

By chance and charm, we agreed to meet
after recess one winter afternoon.

Cold, and hovering quietly,
perfectly still, we waited to be alone.

Eddie grinned and reached for my hand
as the door sealed the darkness inside.

Puffy coats, mittens, and scarves
gasped at our first kiss.

I Used To

I used to Double-Dutch and smell
        of sweat. Rhythm, alternating legs,
danced in the street, ass and torso pulsing.

As the ropes slapped pavement, I rocked back-and-forth
        synchronized to the tempo. Without hesitation
ready to jump inside, chants and singing.

I used to skip down the sidewalk, catching fireflies.
        My hands cupped together, waiting
to feel the tiny legs relaxed in my palm.

Slowly peeled back my fingers,
        I named the flickering illuminations.
My palms flat open to release.

Sacred

how sorrowful the violin strings ached
as the shallow breath of night faded.
ambient moaning resonated.
bow angled toward the fingerboard.

thick stemmed vines crawl
among the slurred notes.
transporting nightly gusts of sadness.
pulling the deepest sympathy
from the tenderhearted.

a benediction of notes.
arrange emotions echoing
in the instrument's body.
moonlit vines and leaves
small petals tightly spun.

apologize as the crescendo
imposed deep and full
the requiem.

Spirits

Before dawn, the graveyard
is static. A veil of trees
hides the shadows.

Fog fills the air
warning birds
and other creatures.

The dark spirits,
rough and heavy
hover close to earth.

They don't like the cemetery's
edge where cars pass
and the fence partitions worlds.

Some remain stuck, lost.
Irreverent. As if, they aren't
sure what to do.

Soon, the sun will lift the fog
and shift the living
and the dead.

Virginia Avenue

A street signed *Virginia Avenue*
on a pole leaning ever so slightly.
On the sunken curb near an oil-can
and a push lawn mower.

My neighbor walked me,
hand-in-hand, to the corner
where a paperboy sat on a rusty box.

Mr. Gude wore dress pants
with a sleeveless undershirt.
He reached into his pocket,
and pulled out a dime.

In slow motion the dime
spun high in the air.
Shiny and thin, shiny and thin.

Two in the Cemetery

Yesterday, the geese wandered in the cemetery.
Long black necks pecking repeatedly.
Beaks low, searching the dormant grass. Or resting,
their white cheeks nestled near one wing.
Slowly they scattered in different patterns.

Together two, still grazing unhurried,
deliberately waddled downhill
near a path of loose gravel. They passed
an old headstone with faded plastic
flowers and a mound of amber leaves.

Today, a dark truck stopped near the hill.
Two gravediggers, shovels in hands, surveyed
a plot. They looked down studying the
wintry ground. Purposefully scouring
the grass, dirt, dust.

There was something relaxed about their undertaking,
something that reminded me of the geese.

Reflection

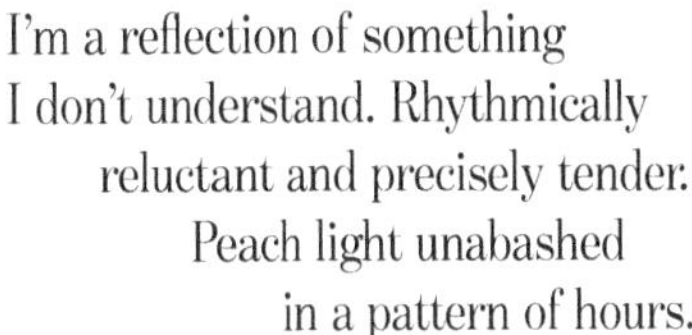

I'm a reflection of something
I don't understand. Rhythmically
    reluctant and precisely tender:
      Peach light unabashed
        in a pattern of hours.

Everything exists outside of me.
Yesterday, I fell in love with silence
    and she was vaguely flattering. Piecing
      me together, flesh, hips and earlobes.
        Calm gentle charms.

As she coaxed evening, I faded
until all that remained were my eyes
    shading ordinary things. A leaf floating
      upward, a silver spool of thread, flecks of dust.
        The universe never dreams of me.

A Pile of Lincoln Logs

A clearing of felled trees.
Scaled bark, unopened cones.

Loamy, acidic ground forms
slender straight trees fifty feet long.

Shallow roots like a restless soul
pressed against a fear.

Lodgepole pine blowdowns
bleak with fading echoes.

Timber crashing down like Lincoln Logs,
scattered acres of ravaged piles.

To live one's entire life, knowing
not the weakness within.

The July Heat

The July heat never escaped the city blocks
asphalt and brick. Kind of like us, stuck
in that time, that place. William
was too awkward, too smart
for a sixteen-year-old.

Some nights, William would climb up my porch,
lift himself on the wrought iron post, and scale
the last five feet of my second-floor balcony.
Two in the morning, he'd walk into my bedroom.
He just wanted to talk, to avoid being alone.

We didn't have money for cigarettes,
it was too hot for that anyway. Flat on our backs
sprawled out on the balcony under the night sky.
The still air hot and heavy against our skin.
We watched the highway roll past.

At two in the morning, the highway slowed
to a waltz. When a car glided past, we would create
an epic tale of freedom, sexy success with a hint
of danger. Airport bound, headed far away
from our apartment flats. We were both dreamers.

William was the awkward one, the smart one.
He was the first to go. The first to escape the July heat.
The first to visit me later—in my dreams.

Needing Him

Sister, you wanted to clean your husband's garage.
Concrete floor, pegboard walls, metal shelves,
with lone light bulbs and overfilled boxes of nails.
Seven electric screwdrivers for others to borrow.

We met for brunch, not discussing the five years of
treatments. Instead, you talked about which memories
to keep and which items to let go. As you unwound the wire
off the spool, so the recycle center will pay more

you looked through me and said, *Near the end
he wasn't able to do much.* He tried to clean his garage once
sat in a metal chair saying yes or no, as you brushed
off dusty tackle boxes, tin trays, relics of his life.

You organized his years in neat piles. On one shelf,
connectors, pliers and wire strippers—waiting,
in case anyone needed them.

Exactly You

There's a photo of you holding me.
I was mesmerized by you, your wispy grey hair,
and thick brows. Your dark eyes fascinated me.

       You held me on your lap while you played cards
and drank sweet tea. Neither of us were comfortable
in that formal world of cloth napkins and lace,
but you bounced me on your leg to make me giggle.

We were more comfortable in the back yard
among sheers that looked like giant scissors.
And I thought it funny how you trimmed
every blade of grass with such precision. Once

       my uncles asked me which one
of them would walk me down the aisle,
and I said you. They told me you wouldn't
live that long, and they were right.

The Loss of a Father

Hamlet saw his father's ghost and went mad;
not allowed to mourn the death, he unraveled.
How can a brute take a loving father from his son?

I.
When I was a child, I didn't know that everyone had a
dad. I thought dads were like aunts, cousins, and step-parents
some kids had them and others did not, but the reality
was that single mothers were my neighborhood and my world.
My father fled incarceration when I was one. I couldn't
understand why he never wanted to meet. Numbness
endured for years. When he died, I mourned
the possibility, not the man.

II.
My husband's father died
when my husband was sixteen.
At sixteen, he wanted to provide for his family.
He refuses to talk about those years now erased.
Sunken grey eyes, watery, blinking.
Refuses to admit the loss, the stress, or the pain.

For our own sons, we pretend to know
what a functioning family might be,
but family isn't intrinsic. Longing
to be close without vulnerability, we
thirst for nostalgia to measure the value of family.

III.
Yet today, I am standing roadside
to watch the funeral procession. The wind
sweeps the leaves in spirals around my feet
perched between a father with two sons and a grandma
waving flags. Across the street uniforms place the coffin.

The hearse stops in front of me. A phone from the back seat
of the limousine records my respect to show the young son
when he is old enough, trying to understand.
How can a brute take a loving
father from the child?
What madness.

Haven't a Name

When I was knee-high, my aunt
told me that my father and his second wife
had a son and a daughter.

But I don't know them.
I don't have their names.
Not an image, or a personality.
We have the same father
but I've never met him.
So I can't say
they have father's eyes.
His disposition. His insensibility.

I have a faint feeling of more siblings
from his family number three.
And news of the fourth family
was hushed. Or consider there
might be more.

Maybe someone told them,
in another country,
the first wife had
four children.
Or maybe I don't exist
in their memories or minds.
Maybe I haven't a name,
nor an image, or a being.

Her Working Hands

Mom's veined hands, now
tissue paper skin, loose wrinkles.
Spent dressing wounds and recording vitals.
Reaching out to touch a patient's knee.

Around the house her plumber's
hands, wet with labor, replacing
the flush valve, sealing the damp
basement, or under the car changing the oil.

During rest, there is laundry and cooking.
Sometimes joking, she raises her hands
covering her mouth as laughter spills out.
Mom's hands embracing life.

In My Rocking Chair

In the dark there is peace
    In the light there is warmth
        but no movement.
    The stillness balances
perfectly on the bowed wood.

In my imagination, I see a hint
    of a playful smile. Small tennis shoes
        kick to and fro sporadically.
    The shoulders of the child
rock forward with anticipation.

His cheeks cherry with excitement,
    his soul shines through his eyes. He asks
        Can I play today? I promise
    to be quiet. No one will know
I'm here in your rocking chair.

Conversation With a Friend

I don't know what brought
us to that intersection,
a prelude to pain.
I was driving
when I saw
your bicycle
next to the ambulance.

You were murky dark
blood on the sidewalk
in front of our favorite
Chinese takeout.

The car that hit you, sped away.
Your skin burned, evaporated.
I was holding your head
as blood surged,
gurgled backwash
down your throat.
You couldn't talk
but some part of you,
unburdened, lifted
your stumbling soul out.

Sorrow echoed
inside of me.
My unrecognizable
last words for you,
your mother's son.

Elegy for a Snag

Beyond the parking lot and rusted fence
I mourned the mangled figure.
Loneliness moaned for the once majestic.

Blood flowed, rain pulsed. Snared and decayed,
twisted branches weeping, the beauty haggard.
Selfish fate wounded my gentle angel.

The young flew away dragging bird nests
like a lost man wonders if it was his fault.
The silence of hysteria.

Leave me,
she said,
as her breath
weakened.

I cannot remember my dark queen
in raw, wet grass.
I wanted to be with her.

Long Pause

We were told you,
didn't feel any pain.

Your breathing was peaceful
but so slow. We would
count the seconds your body
took to inhale. Count
the seconds your body
took to exhale.

During the listening
and the counting,
your breathing
would stop.

Nothing in.
Nothing out.
Only a
long pause.

In your hospital room,
eyes searched
for each other.

And our hearts
whispered to our minds.
How many seconds
before your
body started
breathing?

The pauses grew longer
as the night progressed.
I didn't want to stay.
I didn't want to hear.
The long pause
never end.

The Duality

of loneliness and love in my mother's
eyes, somehow existing together.

An inner place with shadows
she is waiting at a wall.

Carrying on her shoulders
a silence.

I'm alone sometimes, but loneliness
without love is different.

A gaping soul carves my insides out of my body
and the me inside echoes around the hollow chamber.

I don't know how to be loved
I don't know how to be loved and to be alone.

I think mothers know,
especially, older mothers.

That's what they live with
a duality of love and loneliness.

Grandma's Piano

It was a snowy day in March.
The century-old piano

needed to be dismantled
to reveal the bare mechanics.

Restore not replace. Strings,
springs, and hammers

in a linear pattern, explained the man.
Keys pounded out discords.

Gently re-strung the bridle tape.
Together, we found the third

missing jack, but my grandma never
played, the only item she left to me.

Unattached

Twenty years ago, we were sitting
on your tailgate drinking beer
after the late shift. I wanted
to let go of something,
your blue eyes captivated me.

You, a quiet touch. Laughing, revealing
the space between your teeth.
I felt less gone, yet unafraid. We
leaned back and gazed at the stars
while listening to "Bohemian Rhapsody".

After midnight, the parking
lot was vacant. The highway
softened to a rumble. Train tracks
curved behind us. Small white
houses circled the side lot.

You were the guy everyone liked,
but alone you became less charming
and more sincere. In between drinking
and talking, I wanted you
without compromise.

Being liked by you was easy,
something I imagined
the beautiful people felt,
but I promised myself I
wouldn't get attached
to anyone.

All Night Listening

to your breathing—my partner, my love, my friend.
    Much like the song of our self, soft melody swirling.
        Whatever you managed to carry from your past lives

emerges with a hum and a sigh drifting on a breeze.
    Spooning your warm body, limbs and skin
        of enchantment. Together, our dreams

float above the trees and sprout delicate wings.
    Think translucent locust shells of three summers past,
        and we can play catch in the damp grass. You

the color of laughter, bright tangerine green
    smirking gently with sleepy eyes.
        Our souls are from midnight.

Unceasing, it's just a voice in my head
    listening to your breathing
        my partner, my love, my friend.

Your Devotion

I should not complain of your genuine
devotion. You believing that I'm worthy
wishing me bewildering success.

You think yourself a wagging
pup. Innocent and pure
beloved by all.

But we are both aware of fate
and luck in the struggle
to survive the self.

While ghosts of insecurity whisper
doubtful phrases, repeating
how undeserving I am.

I should not complain of your excitement
when I walk through the door
and you cannot contain yourself.

We Were Consumed

You were building a campfire,
carefully placing each piece
of dry tinder & kindling.

Hesitantly, you reached
for my hand as clouds cooled
the damp night. Moisture

cracked within the logs.
Your swollen knuckles
locked our fingers together.

Untamed flames jumped,
floating ash & smoke.
The wilderness greying

at your temples. Heat
from the glowing
embers consumed us.

Entering Through a Window

The gangway was shadowed and desolate.
between the next apartment and ours
only dirt, debris, and cement eight feet wide.
On the back most corner, the first-floor window.

I stepped over the coiled hose, placed my foot
on the spigot and thrust my weight.
My right knee scraped against the red, sandy wall.
I hoisted my hip on the outside frame's edge.

I leaned into the pane, reached for the rail,
twisted my wrist and jiggled. Listening for the chain
in the side-jamb, the sash weights released. The lower
double-hung floated up as I exhaled.

Goodnight Everything

The winter wheat waves
to the Midwestern plains.

Weeds in sidewalk cracks
bow to muddy riverbanks.

Draped across the wooden chair,
apron strings crisscross and sigh.

Ceiling rafters chant incantations,
doorknobs and light shades join in.

Under calico blankets, the shadows hush.
The real me fades, longing for, listening for

everything inside my pathetic
chest. I want to weave the sounds

into a vain creation, but the flurried
music vanishes in and out of a haze

until all I hear is everything.

Always Fleeting

Next to the wrinkled
bark and sticky leaves
swallows perch on the
newly budding branches.

They warble gentle
nudges, like a friend that
is not quite gone. Fluttering
in the yard of clay roots
 and rambling memories.

Newly cut grass inviting
the birds to thrust above
the low contour. Foraging,
they flap wind and body.
Wings fold then release.

Lifted flight.

Acknowledgments of Poems

"City Life" first published in UMSL *Litmag* 2018.

"Eating Over the Sink" first published in UCity Review, Issue 17, December 2018.

"The Loss of a Father" first published in UMSL *Litmag* 2019.

"Sunset With a Heron" first published in Littoral Magazine Aug. 2022.

"My Snag"/"Elegy for a Tree" first published in Littoral Magazine Aug. 2022

"Third Generation" *MacGuffin* 39.2 Galleys Fall 2023.

"Where Dreams Take Place" first published in *Glacial Hills Review* 2024.

"One Thing" Cor Jesu Academy Instagram instagram.com/p/DDmt0Pcif5C/?igsh=MWp2OG5wa3pqeXJjeQ%3D%3D

"Needing Him"/"Cleaning his Garage" first published in *Blue Collar Review* 2024.

"Standing in Promises" first published in *The Journal of Undiscovered Poets* Issue 7 2024.

"Splitting Wood" first published in *The San Pedro River Review* 2025.

"Crashing into the Shore", "Reflection", "Grandma's Piano", "In my Rocking Chair" and "All Night Listening" first published in *On the Edge* a collection of Missouri Poetry 2025.

"Spirits", "Viginia Avenue", and "We Were Consumed" forthcoming in Grist (Missouri) 2025.

"Scavenger Finds a Body" forthcoming in *Glassworks Magazine* Spring Issue #32 2026.

About the Author

Andrea is a quiet, quirky teacher and poet from Missouri; *Gentle Haunts* is her debut poetry collection. In 2021 Andrea earned her MFA from the University of Missouri St. Louis. Her work has appeared in *The San Pedro River Review*, *The Journal of Undiscovered Poets*, *The Blue Collar Review*, *The Glacial Hill Review*, *MacGuffin*, *UMSL Litmag*, and more. Andrea likes to hike in the Ozarks with her husband, and her latest joy is a 46lb. lap dog named Rigby.

Andrea is available for interviews.

Follow her on social media as **poetandreareynolds**.

Instagram: @poetandreareynolds

Facebook: @poetandreareynolds

Website: poetandreareynolds.com